IS SLAVERY SANCTIONED BY THE BIBLE

By Isaac Allen

If there is one subject which, above all others, may be regarded as of national interest at the present time, it is the subject of Slavery. Wherever we go, north or south, east or west, at the fireside, in the factory, the rail-car or the steamboat, in the state legislatures or the national Congress, this "ghost that will not down" obtrudes itself. The strife has involved press, pulpit, and forum alike, and in spite of all compromises by political parties, and the desperate attempts at non-committal by religious bodies, it only grows wider and deeper.

But the distinctive feature of this, as compared with other questions of national import, is, that here both parties draw their principal arguments from the Bible as a common armory of weapons for attack and defense. On the one side, it is claimed that slavery, as it exists in the United States, is not a moral evil; that it is an innocent and lawful relation, as much as that of parent and child, husband and wife, or any other in society; that the right to buy, sell, and hold men for purposes of gain, was given by express permission of God, and sanctioned by Christ and his apostles; that this right is founded on the golden rule; and says Dr. Shannon of Bacon College, Ky., "I hardly know which is most unaccountable, the profound ignorance of the Bible, or the sublimity of cool impudence and infidelity manifested by those who profess to be Christians; and yet dare affirm that the Book of God gives no sanction to slaveholding." All these affirmations are fairly summed up thus: "As slavery was practiced by the patriarchs, received sanction and legality from God in the Mosaic law, and was not denounced by Christ and his apostles, it must have been right. If right then, it is so still; therefore Southern slavery is right."

On the other hand, it is contended that chattel slavery[Pg 2] is nowhere warranted or sanctioned by the Bible, but is totally opposed both to its spirit and teachings.

It will be the object of the present discussion to determine which of these opinions is correct.

SLAVERY DEFINED.

What, then, is chattel slavery as understood in American law?

1. It is not the relation of wife or child. In one sense a man may be said to "possess" these; but he can not buy or sell them. These are natural relations; and he who violates them for the sake of gain is branded by all as barbarous and criminal.

2. Not the relation of apprentice or minor. This is temporary, having for its primary object, not the good of the master or guardian, but that of the apprentice or minor, his education and preparation for acting his part as a free and independent member of society; but

chattelism is life bondage, for the sole good of the master.

3. Not the relation of service by contract. Here a bond or agreement is implied, and therefore reciprocal rights, and the mutual power of dissolution on failure of either in the terms of mutual agreement; but chattelism ignores and denies the ability of the slave to make a contract.

4. Not serfdom or villeinage. The serf or villein was attached to the glebe or soil, and could not be severed from it, deprived of his family, or sold to another as a chattel; being retained as part of the indivisible feudal community. But the chattel slave is a "thing" incapable of family relations, and may be sold when, where, or how the master pleases.

Chattelism is none of these relations; its principle is "property in man." Its definition is thus given in the law of Louisiana, (Civil Code, art. 35:) "A slave is one who is in the power of his master, to whom he belongs. The master may sell him, dispose of his person, his industry, his labor; he can do nothing, possess nothing, acquire nothing, but what must belong to his master."

South Carolina says, (Prince's Digest, 446,) "Slaves shall be deemed, sold, taken, reputed, and adjudged in law, to be chattels personal in the hands of their owners and possessors, and their executors, administrators, and[Pg 3] assigns, to all intents, purposes, and constructions whatsoever."

Judge Ruffin, giving the opinion of the Supreme Court of North Carolina, (case of State v. Mann,) says a slave is "one doomed in his own person and his posterity to live without knowledge, and without the capacity to make any thing his own, and to toil that another may reap the fruits."

We now come to the point at issue: Does the Bible sanction this system?

OLD TESTAMENT.

1. Hebrew Terms.

The Hebrew terms used in reference to this subject are ?????, auvadh, "to serve;" the noun, ?????, evedh, "servant" or "bondman," one contracting service for a term of years; ????????, saukir, a "hired servant" daily or weekly; ?????, aumau, and ????????, shiphechau, "maid-servant" or "handmaid;" but there is no term in Hebrew synonymous with our word slave, for all the terms applied to servants are, as we shall show, equally applicable and applied to free persons.

The verb ?????, auvadh, according to Gesenius, signifies primarily, to labor; then, to labor for one's self, for hire, or compulsory labor as a captive or prisoner of war. Gen. 2:5, 15; 3:23; 29:15. Ex. 20:9; 21:2. Next, national servitude as tributary to others; as

Sodom and the cities of the plain to Chedorlaomer, Gen. 14:4; Esau to Jacob, Gen. 25:23; the Israelites in Canaan to surrounding nations, Moabites, Philistines, and others, Judg. 3:8; Jer. 27:7, 9. Next, national and personal servitude or serfdom, as of the Israelites in Egypt. Lastly, the service of God or idols, Judg. 3:7, &c. From these and similar passages we see that neither the generic nor specific meaning of the term, taken in its connections, implies chattel slavery, but labor, voluntary, hired, or compulsory, as of tributary nations or prisoners of war, whose claim to regain, if possible, their freedom and rights, is ever admitted and acted on; showing that freedom is the normal state of man, subjection and compulsory servitude the abnormal and unnatural.[Pg 4]

But it is objected that, though the proper meaning of the verb "to serve" does not imply chattel slavery, it is certain that the derived noun ?????, evedh, translated "servant" and "bondman" in our version, is frequently used to designate involuntary servitude, the service of one "bought with money," and therefore a chattel slave. We reply, By far the most frequent use of this term, as is well known, represents either the common deferential mode of address of inferiors to superiors, or equals to equals, used then and to-day in the East, or the political subordination of inferior to superior rank invariably existing in Eastern governments. Otherwise we have Jacob saying to Esau, "The children which God hath graciously given thy" slave;

and Joseph's brethren saying to him, "Thou saidst to thy slaves, Bring him down to me." "When we came up to thy slave my father." Saul's officers and soldiers are his slaves, David is Jonathan's, and vice versa; Abigail, David's wife, is his slave; his people, officers, and even embassadors are all his slaves; all are slaves to each other, and none are masters, unless it be the king.

How, then, can we properly define the meaning and status of the term "servant" in any particular passage? We answer, only by the context and the usage of the particular time and place, so far as known.

2. The Curse of Canaan.

We first meet with the term "servant" in the oft-disputed passage, Gen. 9:25-27: "Cursed be Canaan; a servant of servants shall he be unto his brethren.... Blessed be the Lord God of Shem, and Canaan shall be his servant." ... Now, as we have no state of servitude in the context or the usage of the times with which to compare this, and as only Canaan and his descendants are included in the curse, we must look to their subsequent history for the fulfillment of the prophecy, and the kind of servitude there implied.

We find the descendants of Canaan and their land defined in Gen. 10:15-20. They were not the Africans, as some ignorantly assert, but the Canaanites, who dwelt in Canaan, and were there destroyed by the Israelites, or rendered tributaries, except the

Gibeonites, who were doomed to be "hewers of wood and drawers of water,"[Pg 5] the serfs of the temple service. Josh. 9:23, 27. There is not one word of buying and selling individuals—no chattelism, or any sanction of it; there is a performing of the service of the temple, or paying tribute, but never slaves or chattels. Canaan thus became the servant (not slave) of Shem; and when afterward Israel was oppressed and rendered tributary to other nations, the Canaanites became thus not only "servants," but "servants of servants."

3. Patriarchal Servitude.

The next example of the word "servant" brings us to that epoch in relation to which the Harmony Presbytery of South Carolina says, "Slavery has existed from the days of those good old slaveholders Abraham, Isaac, and Jacob, (who are now in the kingdom of heaven,) to the time when the apostle Paul sent a runaway home to his master Philemon, and wrote a Christian and paternal letter to this slaveholder, which we find still stands in the canon of the Scriptures."

The account we have of Abraham's servants is briefly as follows: That he had men-servants and maid-servants, Gen. 12:16; 14:14; 17:27, (not slaves, for we have shown above by numerous passages that to give such a definition to the term "servant" is false and absurd, unless sustained by the context or the usage of the times;) that they numbered some two thousand persons, (reckoning by the number of fighting men among them, generally one in five of the population,) were trained and accustomed to arms, Gen. 14:14; could inherit property, Gen. 15:3, 4; in religious ordinances were perfectly equal with the master, Gen. 17:10-14; had entire control not only over the property, but also the heirs of the household, Gen. 24:2-10; lastly, they were invariably considered as men, not slaves or chattels. Gen. 24:30, 32. "And the man (servant of Abraham) came into the house, and he ungirded his camels, and gave straw and provender for the camels, and water to wash his feet and the men's feet that were with him."

"But," it is objected, "some of these servants were 'bought with money;' therefore they must have been possessed as 'chattel slaves.'" This conclusion depends[Pg 6] partly on the meaning of the Hebrew verb ?????, kaunau, "to buy;" and asserts that whenever this term is applied to persons, it implies the relation of chattel slavery. The primary definition of the verb, given by Gesenius, is, to erect; then, 1. To found or create; 2. To get, gain, obtain, acquire, possess; 3. To get by purchase, to buy.

Let us see the meaning of this term, applied to persons in other passages. In Gen. 31:15, Rachel and Leah say of their father, "He hath sold us, and quite devoured also our money," referring to Jacob's long service for them; were they chattels? Gen. 47:23, Joseph bought the Egyptians; were they chattels? Ex.

21:2, "If thou buy a Hebrew servant, six years shall he serve, and in the seventh he shall go out free, for nothing;" was he a chattel? Ruth 4:10, "Ruth the Moabitess have I purchased this day to be my wife;" was she a chattel? These passages clearly show that the simple application of the term "bought with money" does not imply property and possession as a chattel.

The phrase "bought with money" relates, in the case of wives, to the dowry usual in Eastern countries; in the case of servants, to the ransom paid for captives in war, and paid by the individual on adoption into the tribe; or to an equivalent paid as hire of time and labor for a limited period, either to parents for their children as apprentices, &c., or to the individual himself, as Jacob to Laban. Gen. 31:41, "Thus have I been twenty years in thy house; I served thee fourteen years for thy two daughters, and six years for thy cattle, and thou hast changed my wages ten times." Thus Abraham could acquire a claim on the service of a man during life by purchase from himself; could acquire the allegiance of a man and his family, and all born in it, by contract, not to be broken but by mutual agreement; and in a few years have a vast household under his authority, "born in his house," and "bought with money," yet not one of them a slave.

Another general proof already alluded to is, that the terms ?????, "servant," and ?????, naar, "young man," are applied synonymously and equally to servants and free persons. Gen. 14:24, Abraham calls his servants young men, and again in Gen. 17:23, 27. So in Job 1:15-19, the term ????? is applied alike to Job's servants and sons. [Pg 7] Also in Judg. 7:10; 19:3, 11, 19; 1 Sam. 9:3, 5, 10, 22, and numerous other places, these terms are applied indiscriminately to servants, showing that they were always regarded as men, never as chattels.

But we are not left to conjecture in regard to the status or condition of Abraham's servants; we will bring proofs showing that it could not have been chattel slavery.

Two of the fundamental characteristics of chattelism are, The status of the mother decides that of the child, and The slave, being property, can not inherit or possess property. Was this the condition of "servants" in patriarchal society? If so, then these characteristics brand them as chattels; but on the contrary, if no record is found of their being sold, (the buying we have already reasonably accounted for;) if the children of these servants were reckoned free, if they and their children could inherit property, then even American slave law and custom declare them free persons, and not chattels personal.

Take the case of Hagar. We read, Gen. 16:1, she was an Egyptian "handmaid, maid-servant," perhaps one of those referred to in Gen. 12:16. Abraham, at Sarah's instigation, makes her his concubine. The usual bickering of Eastern harems ensues. Hagar leaves the tribe, is sent back by the angel, Ishmael is born, and this son of a slave (?) is regarded not only as free, but heir of the house of Abraham. Years pass, and the wild, reckless Ishmael is seen ridiculing Isaac, his puny brother and coheir. At the sight, all the mother and the aristocrat again rise up in Sarah, and she cries out to Abraham, "Cast out this bondwoman and her son, for he shall not be heir with my son, even Isaac;" and Abraham, so far from regarding them as chattels personal, and selling them south, sends off the wild boy to be the wild, free Arab, "whose hand will be against every man, and every man's hand against his."

Take the case of Bilhah and Zilpah, given by Laban (Gen. 29:24, 29,) as handmaids (?????) to his daughters Leah and Rachel. Gen. 30:4-14. They become Jacob's concubines, and bear him four sons—Dan, Naphtali, Gad, and Asher. Here the case is plain; the mothers are "servants," they have children, and these, instead of being (as in similar cases daily at the South)[Pg 8] "reputed and adjudged in law to be chattels personal," are recognized as free and equal with the other sons, Reuben, Judah, &c., and become, like them, heads of tribes in Israel. In these cases,—and they are all which relate to the point at issue,—either the status of these servants did or did not decide that of their children. If it did, then, by the laws of chattelism, the children being free prove the mother (though servant) to be free; if it did not, then the mother was held only by feudal allegiance, while the children were always free. In either case the conditions of chattelism did not exist; they were not slaves, but free persons in the same condition as members of wandering Arab and Tartar tribes to this day.

Did the second fundamental condition of chattelism mentioned above exist? The slave, being property, can not possess or inherit property. In Gen. 15:3 we find Abraham complaining to the Lord, "Behold, to me thou hast given no seed, and lo, one born in my house is my heir!" The same term is used here as in speaking of Abraham's other servants; and yet this "servant" is declared by Abraham his acknowledged heir. Here there is a manifest contradiction of the conditions of a chattel slave. They can not inherit property; this man could; therefore he was not a slave. It is an entirely gratuitous assumption to assert that Abraham's dependents were slaves; for similar cases occur daily in nomadic tribes, as formerly they did in Scottish clans. If the chief has no child capable of succeeding him in office, he chooses from his dependents some tried and trusty warrior, and adopts him as lieutenant or henchman, to succeed him as heir or chief. Just so Abraham, then nearly eighty years old, despairing of a son to take his place as chief of the tribe, adopted some young warrior (perhaps a leader in the battle of Hobah) as his heir, with the proviso of resigning in favor of a son if any be born. But in the case of Jacob's four sons the conclusion is self-evident—children of "servants" or "handmaids," yet recognized as free like the other sons, sharing the property of the father equally with them;—the conditions of a state of chattelism did not exist.

These things prove conclusively that the term "servant" never meant slave in patriarchal families; that the[Pg 9] term "bought with money" referred only to feudal allegiance or service for a time agreed on by both parties. These servants could possess and inherit property; their children were free; they were trained to the use of arms; in religious matters master and servant were alike and equal; and they were always considered and called men, never slaves or chattels,—all which are directly contrary to the principles and express enactments of American slave law, and are the characteristics of free persons even at the South. Add to this the significant fact that not one word is said in the patriarchal records of selling any of these servants, (the only act mentioned of selling a human being is that of Joseph by his brethren, so bitterly reprobated and repented of by them soon after,) though frequently bought; that no fugitive law existed, in fact could not exist in a wandering tribe,—and the natural conclusion is, that they were not slaves, but free men and women; and therefore the records of patriarchal society conclusively deny the existence of chattel slaves or slavery as one of its institutions.

Years pass, and we find the Israelites reduced to a servile condition as the serfs of the Egyptians. God, in his purposes, allowed them to remain thus for a time, and then, instead of sanctioning even this modified form of slavery, demanded their instant release; and on refusal, with terrible judgments on their oppressors, he led forth that army of fugitive slaves, and drowned their pursuers in the Red Sea.

4. Mosaic Laws.

We come next to the sanction and authority of chattel slavery claimed to exist in the laws and economy of these people just escaped from bondage, and framed by him who had shown his displeasure against slavery by nearly destroying a nation of slaveholders for holding and catching slaves. The arguments for this claim are—1. That the term "servant" or "bondman" used in the Mosaic law means chattel slavery; 2. That in certain cases the Hebrews might hold their brethren as slaves for ever; 3. They might buy slaves from the heathen around, and hold them for ever. These positions, we admit, have some plausibility, and have doubtless had great weight in producing the opinion that chattelism is sanctioned by the[Pg 10] Bible. We propose to consider the condition of the classes of servants referred to in their order.

1. Hebrew servants. These were of four kinds—servants under contract or indenture for six years, probably from one sabbatic year to another: servants

held till the year of jubilee, or "for ever:" children born in the house, or hired out by their parents: convicted thieves; and afterward, though sanctioned by no law, debtors.

In respect to the first of these classes, the law is found in Ex. 21:2-6; Deut. 15:12-18. "If thou buy a Hebrew servant, six years shall he serve, and in the seventh he shall go out free, for nothing." Here the term "buy" can only be applied to the service, sold by the servant for six years, (or perhaps to the sabbatic seventh year, as daily or weekly service ended with the Sabbath,) for it is applied to a state which no ingenuity whatever can construe as chattelism.

The second class of Hebrew servants is mentioned Ex. 21:5, 6. "If the servant shall plainly say, I love my master, my wife, and my children; I will not go out free; then his master shall bring him to the judges: he shall also bring him to the door or to the door-post, and he shall bore his ear through with an awl, and he shall serve him for ever." Deut. 15:17, the same law adds, "And also to thy maid-servant shalt thou do likewise." But in Lev. 25:39, 40, 53, it is expressly enacted that one who served longer than six years was not to be treated or considered as an ?????, evedh, one contracting for a term of years, but as a ????????, saukir, a hired servant, to be well treated and compensated for his services. "Thou shalt not compel him to serve as a bond-servant, but as a hired servant and as a sojourner he shall be with thee." The servant must plainly say, "I will not go out;" it must be voluntary service; but chattelism is involuntary, forced, and directly contrary to the case before us. "He shall serve him for ever," not his sons after him, not giving the right of transfer or sale of service to a third person, "He shall serve," not his wife or children, but himself, till death, or his master's death, or the jubilee. This, then, was not chattelism, for it was voluntary, without purchase or sale, ending with the life of the servant, the master, or the year of release—the jubilee.[Pg 11]

The third class of servants—children—appear during minority to have been, as now in all Eastern countries, entirely at the service or control of their parents, and might by them be hired out, Neh. 5:2-6, but, when of age, were of course independent of parental acts and control. John 9:21. That the offspring of servants in patriarchal times were free we have already proved; that they were so among the Israelites is shown by the case of Abimelech, the son of a maid-servant, Judg. 9:18, yet free as his brethren, and afterward king of Israel; also of Sheshan. 1 Chr. 2:34, 35. No service, indeed, could be recognized or demanded, in Jewish law, of grown persons, except as the result of contract or crime.

In respect to the fourth class, it is plain from the language used that only sufficient service could be required of them to cancel the obligation of restitution. Ex. 22:3. "He should make full restitution;

if he have nothing, then he shall be sold for his theft;" in case of debt, Matt. 18:34, "till he should pay all that was due to him."

2. Servants obtained from the heathen. These were, first, captives. From the account of the first taking of captives by the Israelites, Num. 31:7-47, we learn, verse 7, that they marched into Midian, slew all the males, and seized the women, children, flocks, and herds. On their return Moses reprimanded them for disobeying God's command by preserving the grown women; and thereupon they killed all but the virgins and children, reserving them for adoption into the families of the nation. In Deut. 20:14 and 21:10-14, we have these commands and regulations given, with an express prohibition of the enslavement of these captives, in case of repudiation by the captors. "It shall be, if thou have no delight in her, then thou shalt let her go whither she will; but thou shalt not sell her at all for money; thou shalt not make merchandise of her, because thou hast humbled her." Now, all slaveholding tribes and nations, when they seize captives for slaves, aim to obtain as many strong and vigorous men as possible; must it not, therefore, fairly be inferred from this regulation that God, by prohibiting instead of sanctioning the most productive mode of slave-making,—the enslavement of prisoners[Pg 12] of war,—did not intend, but positively prohibited, the Israelites from becoming a slaveholding nation?

Secondly, "bought with money." The law referring to these is Lev. 25:44, 46. "Both thy bondmen and thy bondmaids which thou shalt have shall be of the heathen round about you; of them shall ye buy bondmen and bondmaids.... And ye shall take them as an inheritance for your children after you, to inherit them for a possession; they shall be your bondmen for ever." As we have already stated, the Hebrews had but two terms for "servant"—the generic term evedh, one under contract for a term of years, and saukir, one hired by the day, week, or year. Now, the term here translated "bondman" is the generic ?????, evedh, elsewhere translated "servant," and therefore should have been thus translated here, unless a different rendering is required by the context. The more literal reading of the Hebrew is, "And thy men-servants and thy maid-servants which shall be to thee from the nations around you, of them shall ye procure the man-servant and maid-servant." What, then, was the difference between the Hebrew and heathen evedh?

This. The Hebrew could only be an evedh, a servant by contract, for six years, Ex. 21:2—"Six years shall he serve, but in the seventh he shall go out free;" (longer service could not be contracted for, but must be voluntary, Ex. 21:5;) or as a hired servant or sojourner till the jubilee, but never beyond. Lev. 25:10, 39-41. But a heathen could bind himself as an evedh for longer than six years; and thus his service, unlike the Hebrew, could be "bought" as "an inheritance for your children after you," but, like the Hebrew voluntary "for ever" servants, they were bondmen for the longest time known by the law—till death or the jubilee.

Is it objected that the terms "buy," "possession," "for ever," are used, and indicate chattelism? We answer, All admit the Hebrew was not a chattel; for his service expired at the seventh year, the death of himself or his master. "He shall serve him for ever;" but, if both lived on, this service, though voluntary, as has been shown, expired with all such claims at the jubilee. Since the same terms, and, as we shall show directly, the[Pg 13] jubilee, applied equally to both, if it does not prove the one a chattel, it does not the other; therefore both are equally voluntary contractors. The service, and not the bodies, were bought; and both were equally free at the jubilee.

Two objects were accomplished by this law. 1st. To permit the Hebrews to obtain that assistance in tilling the land, which otherwise they would not have been allowed to do. 2d. To increase the numbers of the commonwealth, since the Hebrews, in obedience to the Abrahamic covenant, Gen. 17:10-14; Ex. 12:44-49, were bound to circumcise these indented servants "bought with money," thus making them part of the household during their period of service, and also naturalized citizens of the state, members of the congregation, partakers of all the rites and privileges common to the mass of the people. Ex. 12:44-9. Num. 15:15-30, "One ordinance shall be both for you of the congregation, and also for the stranger that sojourneth with you, an ordinance for ever in your generations; as ye are, so shall the stranger be before the Lord." Lev. 19:34, "The stranger that dwelleth among you shall be as one born among you, and thou shalt love him as thyself." In accordance with the frequently-repeated injunction of this law of equality, they were invariably recognized as citizens, and alike with Hebrew servants, were amenable to, and received protection from, the laws of the state.

In further proof of this, and in direct opposition to chattelism, is the fact, that the laws regulating the relation of master and servant are each and all enacted for the benefit and protection of the servant, and not one for that of the master. Again, when property is spoken of, oxen, sheep, &c., the term owner is always used, master never; when servants and masters are spoken of, master is always used, owner never. Ex. 21:29, "The ox shall be stoned, and his owner also shall be put to death," Ex. 21:34, If an ox or ass fall into a pit left uncovered, "the owner of the pit shall make it good, and give money to the owner of them." But, Deut. 25:15, "Thou shall not deliver to his master the servant which is escaped from his master unto thee."

The inference from all this is plain. No such thing as[Pg 14] property in man is recognized in the Mosaic law; but God, finding polygamy and the law of serfdom existing among the Israelites, did not see fit to abolish them at once, but so hampered and hedged them about by restrictive statutes as gradually and finally to abolish them altogether.

5. Restrictive Laws.

But lest oppression should trample upon the rights of the laboring classes, and aim at their enslavement,—which actually happened afterward, and was one of the principal items of God's indictment (Jer. 22:3; 34:8-22) against the Jews prior to their destruction by Nebuchadnezzar,—three special enactments were made to prevent such iniquity, and break up any attempt at chattel slavery in the nation.

First. The law against kidnaping.—Ex. 21:16, "He that stealeth a man and selleth him, or if he be found in his hand, he shall surely be put to death." Thus the one great means of obtaining slaves is forbidden. He who (no matter where) seizes a human being, (no matter whom,) and reduces him to involuntary servitude, shall die; for he seeks to take away the rights and privileges of freedom, all that goes to make up life; seeks to make property of man, to extinguish the man in the chattel.

"But," it is said, "this only refers to stealing slaves." Mark the logic: a man could seize and enslave another with impunity; but if, afterward, the father, brother, or friend of the enslaved should attempt to rescue him, he must die! Glorious argument for slaveholders and slave-catchers! It is also said this refers to Hebrews, not strangers. Let God answer. Lev. 24:22, "Ye shall have one manner of law, as well for the stranger as for one of your own country; for I am the Lord your God." This is his interpretation of the breadth of the law given in the preceding verse, "He that killeth a man, he shall be put to death." The law, therefore, is unrestricted and universal; Hebrew or heathen, he that killeth a man and he that stealeth a man shall alike die; thus putting slavery and murder on the same footing, as equally criminal. Now, if God sanctioned slavery, why did he make such an inconsistent law as this forbidding it?[Pg 15]

Second. The law concerning fugitives.—Deut. 23:15, 16, "Thou shalt not deliver to his master the servant which is escaped from his master unto thee; he shall dwell with thee, even among you in that place which he shall choose in one of thy gates where it liketh him best; thou shalt not oppress him."

There is no equivocation here; "thou shalt not deliver unto his master." It is imperative; they were to receive him among them as a citizen, and, if need be, protect him from his master; mark, not a "heathen" or "Hebrew," servant, but the "servant," heathen or

Hebrew, whoever should fly from the ill treatment or injustice of a hard master. Compare for a moment the Hebrew and American fugitive laws. The Hebrew says, "Thou shalt not deliver to his master the servant that is escaped." The American says, "Thou shalt deliver him up to his master, or be fined one thousand dollars, and suffer six months' imprisonment." The Hebrew says, "He shall dwell with thee ... thou shalt not oppress him." The American law says, "The commissioner who tries the case shall get five dollars if he fails, and ten if he succeeds in 'delivering to his master' the fugitive, on the simple affidavit of the former that he is his slave."

What are the deductions from this law of Moses? The return of stray property is expressly commanded in Deut. 22:1-3; the return of servants is expressly forbidden here; the servant could leave a hard master at any time, and the state could not compel him to return: it did not recognize the condition of forced, but only voluntary servitude, and thus rendered the existence of chattelism impossible.

The third great protective law was that of the Jubilee.—Lev. 25:10-55, "And ye shall hallow the fiftieth year, and proclaim liberty throughout all the land unto all the inhabitants thereof; it shall be a jubilee unto you, and ye shall return every man unto his possession, and ye shall return every man to his family." ... Here the expression is emphatic, no reservations are made, no restrictions allowed. As the sound of ??????, ??????, Yoval, Yoval, sounded through the land, and was echoed back from hill and village, from hamlet and town, the cry was taken up, and borne along by the laboring thousands of Israel, many of whom had been toiling under contract for years, by the[Pg 16] unfortunate debtor, and those whom poverty had compelled to part with "the old house at home," all returned, all were free. "Liberty, liberty!"

It is vain to assume that the benefits of the Jubilee were restricted to a particular class. To what class? Not the six years' servants; they were freed in the seventh. Not to debtors; there was no law compelling them to serve at all; therefore they could only serve voluntarily to pay their debts. Not to thieves; they could only be compelled to make restitution of the thing stolen, or its value; that paid, they were free. The only other classes to whom the law could apply were "all the inhabitants of the land" who served the longest time, the Hebrew "for ever" servants, and the heathen servants, thus preventing the possibility of the rise and growth of a servile class, the curse of any country. In this way only can we account for the fact that Jewish history never mentions the existence of a large servile class, or a servile insurrection in Israel, so common and disastrous an occurrence in the history of ancient slaveholding communities.

Some object here, that the term "inhabitants" implies "all the Hebrews," and excludes the strangers, Canaanites, &c.; but by admitting that "all the Hebrews" were freed at the Jubilee, they admit that those who, in Ex. 21:6, are servants "for ever," are also freed, and thus to serve "for ever" only implies till the Jubilee. If, then, "for ever" means only till the Jubilee in one case, it means no more in the other. And if we show that the strangers and Canaanites were considered "inhabitants of the land," then the Jubilee referred to Hebrew and stranger alike, and both were free. In Ex. 34:12, 15, "Take heed to thyself, lest thou make a covenant with the inhabitants of the land whither thou goest;" and Lev. 18:25; Num. 33:52-55, Moses calls the heathen "the inhabitants of the land;" and as he was likely to understand the meaning of the term pretty well, he either refers in the Jubilee law to Hebrews, Canaanites, and all, or he meant Canaanites and heathen alone, which is still more decisive. Again, in 2 Sam. 11:2-27; 23:39, we find one of these strangers, Uriah the Hittite, not only an "inhabitant" of Jerusalem, but one of David's best officers, and his wife becoming queen of Israel and mother of Solomon; and in 2 Sam. 24:18-25, another, Araunah[Pg 17] the Jebusite is a householder, and more, is praised as acting like a king toward king David, who bought property of him whereon to build an altar; and yet, forsooth, they were not inhabitants!

But, as if to prevent equivocation, Moses defines the phrase "all the inhabitants;" "Ye shall return every man to his possession, and ye shall return every man to his family." Not every Hebrew, but every man, the same generic term as in the law against killing or stealing "a man;" it is unqualified and universal. Thus with one blow this noble law strikes down the two principal sources of social oppression—monopoly of land and monopoly of labor. All who had by poverty been compelled to part with the old farm and homestead received it back; all claims of service against any person, however mean and humble, were canceled; and the land and its inhabitants were again free as God had made them.

These accumulated arguments, each separately weighty and forcible, but collectively insurmountable, we think prove conclusively that the form of servitude among the Israelites was not chattel slavery, and that there is no sanction or authority for it in the Mosaic laws and regulations.

Thus in Jewish history we see the Israelites groaning under Egyptian bondage, and God's arm outstretched to rescue them when fugitives, and punish their pursuers—a warning to all such thereafter; we see laws enacted to prevent the existence of chattelism among them, by restricting the master's power, and securing the servant's freedom at regular intervals, and the opposite doctrine of equality among men asserted; we see the Israelites disobeying these commands, and adopting, with the idolatry of their neighbors, their slavery also, and God's fiery wrath denounced on them for it by Isaiah, Jeremiah, and Ezekiel, and fulfilled by Nebuchadnezzar in the destruction and captivity of the state.

NEW TESTAMENT.

Teachings of Christ.

Ages pass, the Jews are restored to their land, but the Roman eagle overshadows it and all the civilized world. Despotism is enthroned; and the idea that the world and[Pg 18] its people are the property of Rome and its citizens is questioned only in murmuring whispers. All the relations of Roman life partake of this idea of absolutism; slavery is every where, liberty nowhere. Then the glad tidings of Messiah's coming is announced to an expectant world. Whom will he side with—the crushed and despairing millions, or the aristocratic and haughty few? Will he adopt and develop the idea of equality found in Jewish law, or the principle now ascendant,—"Might makes right,"—the Roman slave law? Let him answer.

Standing in the synagogue at Nazareth, the home of his boyhood, amid his expectant friends and relations, he reads (Luke 4:16-21) from Isaiah, "The spirit of the Lord is upon me, because he hath anointed me to preach the gospel to the poor; he hath sent me to heal the broken-hearted, to preach deliverance to the captives, and recovering of sight to the blind, to set at liberty them that are bruised, to preach the acceptable year of the Lord. And he closed the book and sat down, ... and began to say to them, This day is this scripture fulfilled in your ears." There is his commission and the constitution of his kingdom. Can any thing be more explicit?

Christ himself comes with glad tidings for the poor, to destroy slavery and oppression, and establish liberty. Rejoice, ye poor, taught hitherto that ye were made only for the service of the rich; there is glad tidings for you. Rejoice, captives and slaves, "bruised" with the lash and fetter; God comes "to preach deliverance to the captives, liberty to them that are bruised, and the acceptable year (the Jubilee) of the Lord."

How did he fulfill this commission and pledge? No code of laws and dogmas, terse and dry, were issued by him for the government of his kingdom; but the great principle was proclaimed of a common brotherhood as children of God our Father, and of love to him as such. In his sermon on the mount, the parables of the lost sheep and silver piece, the good Samaritan, the prodigal son, the Pharisee and the publican; in his private teachings to his disciples; and, above all, by his daily example he taught and illustrated, as the leading characteristics of his kingdom, love to God, the brotherhood of man, the rights of all, however poor, degraded, or despised.

More, he[Pg 19] makes this idea of brotherhood and equality even with himself, the great test in the judgment. Matt. 25:40, 45: "And the king shall answer, and say unto them, Verily I say unto you, Inasmuch as ye have done it unto the least of these my brethren, ye have done it unto me." What will those who now boast of their large churches, composed almost entirely of slaves, Christian ministers, and church members, bought, sold, lashed, and treated like cattle, answer the King in that great day?

But to return: the result of such teachings was soon evident. "The common people heard him gladly," hung on his steps and words by thousands, and hailed him as deliverer; while Scribes and Pharisees, priests and rulers, denounced him as "a friend of publicans and sinners," only seeking popularity among the masses, to disturb the public peace, and revolutionize the government. Mark, it was not simply religious, but political interference and teaching they charged him with, and on this charge they finally compassed his death.

In his private teachings to his disciples he strongly inculcated this truth. Striving among themselves for the supremacy, he charges them, Matt. 20:26-28, and many other places, "It shall not be so among you; but whosoever will be chief among you, let him be your servant; even as the Son of man came not to be ministered to, but to minister, and to give his life a ransom for many." The law thus explicitly laid down, and in John 13 enforced by his example, is the very opposite of chattelism. In his church, none were to claim supremacy over others, much less enslave them; none to despise labor and the laborer, much less condemn others to it while themselves lived in idleness.

Thus Christ, so far from sanctioning chattelism or property in man in any shape or form, by precept and example taught the opposite, the dignity of labor and the laborer, the common brotherhood of man, and consequent equality, political and religious. Did his apostles indorse this doctrine, or, fearing the result, did they side with the all prevalent system of class legislation and slavery?

Teachings of the Apostles.

The result of their teaching in Judea is given in Acts 4:32-35—"And the multitude of them that believed[Pg 20] were of one heart and one soul; neither said any of them that aught of the things he possessed was his own; but they had all things common. Neither was there any among them that lacked; for as many as were possessors of lands or houses sold them, and brought the prices of the things that were sold and laid them down at the apostles' feet, and distribution was made to every man according as he had need." They not only believed in "liberty, equality, and fraternity," but practised its extreme—not only equality of rights, but equality of property, among the brotherhood.

But this was comparatively easy in Judea, where the principle of equality was already partly recognized, and the existence of chattelism prevented by the action of the Mosaic code. The apostles only fairly came in conflict with the spirit of caste and slavery when, filled with love and the Spirit, they entered heathen countries, "preaching the glad tidings of the kingdom," and establishing every where the glorious brotherhood of humanity, whose primary law is, "A new commandment I give unto you, That ye love one another as I have loved you. By this shall men know that ye are my disciples, if ye have love one to another." John 13:34-5. And Paul expounds it to the Gentiles, 1 Cor. 12:13—"For by one Spirit are we all baptized into one body, whether we be Jews or Gentiles, whether we be bond or free, and have been all made to drink into one Spirit." Gal. 3:26-28: "Ye are all the children of God by faith in Christ Jesus; for as many of you as have been baptized into Christ have put on Christ. There is neither Jew nor Greek, there is neither bond nor free, there is neither male nor female; for ye are all one in Christ Jesus." Again, Col. 3:11, "There is neither Greek nor Jew, circumcision nor uncircumcision, barbarian nor Scythian, bond nor free; but Christ is all and in all."

Can language be more express and conclusive than this? The distinctions here dissolved by the waters of baptism, and blended into "one in Christ Jesus," are not, as our southern brethren assert, simply religious, but national, political, and social—slavery, and the spirit of caste and clan which upholds it, alike forbidden, and liberty, equality, and fraternity, social, political, and religious, proclaimed as the rule of Christ's kingdom.[Pg 21]

Principles like these came upon the world like the morning sunlight, scattering the mists of superstitious ignorance, melting the icy pride and selfishness of the mighty, permeating all classes and relations of society with their secret influence, and blending all into one harmonious brotherhood of love and peace. Apparently they were subject as others to the laws of the state, but in secret were bound by stronger ties, and governed by higher, nobler laws, than the world outside dreamed of.

Instead of the Roman law of marriage, regarding the wife as the husband's slave, he must love her as himself; more, as Christ loved the church. Instead of the tyranny on one side, and the retaliating disobedience on the other, of the Roman parental relation, it became the image of our heavenly Father's love, and our trusting obedience to him. The relation of slave, "pro nullo, pro quadrupedo, pro mortuo," (as a nobody, a quadruped, a dead man,) to his master, became the relation of brethren, the one to render true and faithful service, Eph. 6:5, the other never to threaten, Eph. 6:9, much less punish; not to regard them as chattels, as under the Roman law, but to give them just and equal compensation for their service, Eph. 6:9; Col. 4:1, "knowing that ye also have a Master in heaven," "neither is there respect of persons with him." The legal deed of manumission was unnecessary; for as, when master and slave land in England, they may remain connected as master and free servant, never as master and slave, so, on admission into the brotherhood of the church, the waters of baptism, as shown above, dissolved the relation of slavery, and substituted that of freemen and brethren.

Again, believers were members of Christ's body. He dwelt in them; and therefore every indignity and injury done to them was done to him in their person. To enslave, buy, and sell them was to enslave, buy, and sell Christ himself. "Inasmuch as ye have done it unto the least of these my brethren, ye have done it unto me." Who, then, would dare hold a brother Christian as a slave? What! make merchandise of the person of Christ? Never! the cry of Judas would ring around them as they were driven ignominiously from the church.

"Why," it is objected, "did not the apostles preach[Pg 22] immediate emancipation, instead of indorsing slavery by defining its duties—'Servants, obey your masters,' &.? and Paul even sent back a slave." 1. The primary object of the apostles was not simply "to preach liberty to the captives;" this was but a branch of the tree planted "for the healing of the nations."

Their object was to sow the principles of faith, love, justice, and equality, well knowing that, when these took root and flourished, among the first fruit would be "liberty to all the inhabitants of the land." 2. Had this been their great object, they took the best and speediest plan for its accomplishment. Attacking the system directly, the appearance of the Christian missionary would have been the signal for servile war and untold bloodshed, the slave against the master, the poor against the rich; and the heathen rulers, eager for a pretext to crush them, would have denounced them as lighting the torch of rebellion and war; and the further spread of the gospel would have been drowned in the blood of its founders. But they took the very course which God adopted among the Israelites in regard to servitude, not directly prohibiting it, but inculcating principles of social equality and progress, restricting the master's power, and protecting the servant's rights, till, master and slave blended in one, the name of slave was lost in that of Christian. 3. The relation and duties of master and servant are defined by the apostles exactly as they might be to-day in England or the free states—as those of men, never as owner and property; on the contrary, all ownership of man by other than God is expressly denied. 1 Cor. 6:19, 20, "What! know ye not that your body is the temple of the Holy Ghost in you, which ye have of God, and ye are not your own? For ye are bought with a price; therefore glorify God in your body and your spirit, which are God's." There the ownership is clearly asserted; how can man claim it? "Render to Cesar the things that are Cesar's, and to God the things that are God's," lest you be found robbing God himself. Again, 1 Cor. 7:21, 23, "Art thou called, being a servant? care not for it; but, if thou mayst be made free, (d?asa? ?e??s?a?, canst become free,) use it rather." What can be more explicit than this? First, ownership of man is denied even to himself, much more to another. Next, the exhortation to slaves is, if they can[Pg 23] not get free from this great wrong, to bear it as such, but, if they can, "use it rather;" and the reason given is followed by a rule of action to be adopted wherever possible. Verse 23, "Ye are bought with a price; be not ye the servants of men." If this be not express prohibition of chattelism, and command to slaves to free themselves from it, then the language is totally contradictory and unintelligible.

Contrast these laws of Paul with the laws of most of the southern states, forbidding even the master to free his slaves, while states and Congress unite in hounding back to whip and task the poor slave who dares obey that command; nay, offer large rewards for men, even Christian ministers, when attempting to obey it. "But Paul sent back Onesimus to his master, and therefore sanctioned the sending back of fugitives." We answer, there was no sending back at all. Paul, a prisoner, could not send him back: a Jew, he was forbidden by his religion to do so. Deut. 23:15.

It was simply a recommendatory letter sent with Onesimus, returning voluntarily to Colosse and his master. Let us look at the letter. Verse 8 begins, "Wherefore, though I might be much bold in Christ to enjoin thee that which is convenient, yet, for love's sake, I rather beseech thee. I beseech thee for my son Onesimus, ... which in time past was to thee unprofitable, but now profitable to thee and to me; whom I have sent again, ... not now as a servant, but above a servant, a brother beloved," &c. Here Onesimus is described as having been, while heathen, an "unprofitable" trouble to his master, and had either run away or been sent away by him. Converted at Rome, Paul heard his story, and in his letter, instead of thinking he is doing Philemon a favor, has to earnestly "beseech," almost command, his reception as a favor to himself. Not one word of property or right in him, save the right of love as one of the brotherhood. "Not now as a servant, but above a servant, a brother beloved, especially to me, but how much more to thee!" Onesimus had left the "slave" in his heathenism; in Christ he became the "brother" of Philemon and Paul. Instead of sanctioning chattelism, it positively denies it by affirming voluntary service, the equality of men as brethren, to be loved as Christ himself.[Pg 24]

Thus Christ and his apostles, so far from upholding chattelism in their teachings, denounced the ownership of man by any but God, and inculcated its opposite—love, liberty, equality, and fraternity—by precept and example. And subsequent history showed the result.

Christ said of the teachings of the Pharisees, "By their fruits ye shall know them." Apply this test to the teachings of the apostles and the primitive churches in regard to slavery. When they went forth, "darkness covered the earth, and gross darkness the people;" slavery sat enthroned in might over Europe; and the cries of the oppressed millions had only had a hearing on the battle or before the throne of God.

When the Reformation came slavery had disappeared in Europe; and the voice of the people was heard asserting their rights, feebly, indeed, at first, but ever since growing stronger and stronger "as the voice of many waters." What has caused this change?

Historians, Protestant and Catholic, ascribe it to the influence of the church, not by direct emancipatory decrees, but, following the example of God through Moses, by gradually restricting the master's power, and protecting the slave; by girdling the poison tree till it withered and fell, though, sad to say, the ruins still disfigure too much field, of the fair fields of Europe and America.

No fact is more patent in history than the truth expressed by Paul to the Corinthians: "Where the Spirit of the Lord is, there is liberty." The whole tendency of the Bible and true Christianity, direct and indirect, is to the liberty and advancement, never the slavery and degradation, of man; and those who have attempted to shield the monster curse of our country and age with the garb of the gospel may find too late, when that awful voice shall ring in their ears, "Inasmuch as ye have done it unto one of the least of these my brethren, ye have done it unto me," that Christ came not only "to preach deliverance to the captives" and "to set at liberty them that are bruised," but also "the day of vengeance of our God."

AMERICAN TRACT SOCIETY,

28 Cornhill, Boston.

[Pg 25]

EXTRACT FROM MR. O'CONOR'S ARGUMENT

Before the New York Court of Appeals, on the "Lemmon Slave Case."

"I submit most respectfully that the only desire I have manifested here or elsewhere, in reference to the question, has been to draw the mind of the court and the intelligent mind of the American people, to the true question which underlies the whole conflict, and that is the question to which my friend (W. W. Evarts, Esq.) has addressed the best, and, in my judgment, the finest part of his very able argument. * * * My friend denounces the institution of slavery as a monstrous injustice, as a sin, as a violation of the law of God and of the law of man, of natural law or natural justice; and in his argument in another place, he called your attention to the enormity of the result claimed in this case, that these eight persons—and not only they, but their posterity to the remotest time—were, by your Honors' judgment, to be consigned to this shocking condition of abject bondage and slavery. Why, how very small and minute was that presentation of the subject! My friend must certainly have used the microscope or reversed the telescope, when, in seeking to present this question in a striking manner to your Honors' minds, he called your attention to these few persons and their posterity. Why, if your Honors please, our territory embraces at the least estimate three millions of these human beings, who, by our laws and institutions, as now existing in these states, * * * are not only consigned to hopeless bondage throughout their whole lives, but to a like condition is their posterity consigned to the remotest times. * * * It is a question of the mightiest magnitude. But the reason why I call your Honors' attention to its magnitude is this: that you may contemplate it in the connection in which my learned friend has presented it; that it is a sin—a violation of natural justice and the law of God; that it is a monstrous scheme of iniquity for defrauding the laborer of his wages—one of those sins that crieth aloud to[Pg 26] heaven for vengeance; that it is a course of unbridled rapine, fraud, and plunder, by which three millions and their posterity are to be oppressed throughout all time. Now, is it a sin? Is this an outrage against divine law and natural justice? If it be such an outrage, then I say it is a sin of the greatest magnitude, of the most enormous and flagitious character that was ever presented to the human mind. The man who does not shrink from it with horror is utterly unworthy the name of a man. It is no trivial offence, that may be tolerated with limitations and qualifications; that we can excuse ourselves for supporting because we have made some kind of a bargain to support it. The tongue of no human being is capable of depicting its enormity; it is not in the power of the human heart to form a just conception of its wickedness and cruelty. And what, I ask, is the rational and necessary consequence, if we regard it to be thus sinful, thus unjust, thus outrageous?"

Dr. Hopkins, of Newport, being much engaged in urging the sinfulness of slavery, called one day at the house of Dr. Bellamy in Bethlem, Connecticut, and while there pressed upon him the duty of liberating his only slave. Dr. B., who was an acute and ingenious reasoner, defended slaveholding by a variety of arguments, to which Dr. H. as ably replied. At length Dr. Hopkins proposed to Dr. Bellamy practical obedience to the golden rule. "Will you give your slave his freedom if he desires it?" Dr. B. replied that the slave was faithful, judicious, trusted with every thing, and would not accept freedom if offered. "Will you free him if he desires it?" repeated Dr. H. "Yes," answered Dr. Bellamy, "I will." "Call him then." The man appeared. "Have you a good, kind master?" asked Dr. Hopkins. "Oh! yes, very, very good." "And are you happy?" "Yes, master, very happy." "Would you be more happy if you were free?" His face brightened. "Oh! yes, master, a great deal more happy." "From this moment," said Dr. Bellamy, "you are free."